Britain in the Thirties
Resource Book

Contents

Change in the Thirties

There are still many people alive who can remember Britain in the 1930s. Some of them call it the time 'before the war'. Their memories will not all be the same because it was a decade when many things were changing. For some people the changes were good, for others they were bad.

You will have to ask each person you talk to where they were living and what jobs their family had in the 1930s. There were big differences between parts of Scotland, Wales, and the north and south of England.

However, by the end of the 1930s, everyone's lives changed. The Second World War had begun.

These workers lived in Oxford. Morris Motors had opened a brand new factory, building cars. There were plenty of jobs for them. More motor cars brought many changes to Britain's roads.

Find:

♦ the cars.

♦ the factory workers. What are they wearing?

♦ where they keep the car parts.

These photographs show some of the differences. They are all black and white because colour photographs were rare in 1930.

This man came from the north of England. He had a lot of skills but he was still **unemployed**. There were over two million people in Britain who were unemployed in 1930.

♦ Why do you think he was walking about with a notice on his back?

♦ What was he worried about?

We do not know where these farmworkers lived, but we can see that the countryside was changing when this photograph was taken.

♦ Can you see the row of new houses behind the field?

♦ Who do you think lived in them?

I KNOW 3 TRADES
I SPEAK 3 LANGUAGES
FOUGHT FOR 3 YEARS
HAVE 3 CHILDREN
AND NO WORK FOR
3 MONTHS
BUT I ONLY WANT
ONE JOB

Unemployed
To be unemployed was to be out of work.

Made in Britain

Before 1930 more things were made in Britain than they are today. Workers in factories and mills, made clothes, shoes, knives and forks, pottery and china. Most things people used in their homes were made here. British goods were also sold all over the world.

But at the beginning of the 1930s, people abroad could not afford to buy things made in Britain. Factories and shipyards began to suffer from a **slump.**

Shipbuilding

On Clydeside, Tyneside, Merseyside and Belfast shipbuilding was the main industry. Work started on this big ship in Scotland, but when the owners found they could not pay the workers' wages, shipbuilding had to stop.

In some places, eight out of every ten workers found themselves out of work.

What do you think happened to the people working on this ship?

Slump

A period of time when it is difficult to sell things.

Cotton Mills

There were problems in Lancashire too. The cotton mills lost many of their customers. Instead of sending raw cotton to be woven in Lancashire, other countires such as India, China and Japan opened their own cotton mills. These mills had new machinery, while the **looms** in Lancashire were over a hundred years old.

Some millowners asked their workers to go on half-time. Others wanted one person to do the same work that two people usually did.

Look at this picture taken inside the Cotton factory.

♦ What would you say if the millowner asked you to work two or three looms at a time?

♦ What would you do if you were a millowner and you could not find enough customers for the cloth that had been produced?

Loom

A machine which wove raw cotton or wool into cloth.

Coal Mining

Coal was the most important source of power in the 1930s. It was needed for railway engines, to make gas and to provide steam power for factory machines. Most people used coal to heat their homes too.

Working coalmines provided jobs for thousands of workers, and in many areas such as the Rhondda valley in Wales, there was very little other work.

Round the coalmine, usually called the 'pit', miners and their families lived in 'pit' villages like the one above in Abertillery. When the mills and shipyards were working, lots of coal was needed but when factories began to close down, the demand for coal also fell. Pits were closed and miners lost their jobs.

This woman has been picking up coal from the slag heap. She is taking it home to keep the family warm.

♦ Why has the woman got her coal from the slag heap?

♦ Where is she going to put the coal?

Slag heap

A pile of rubbish and bad coal outside a coal mine. All the good coal is taken away first.

Out of Work

The Means Test

By 1932 over three million workers had lost their jobs. In Jarrow the shipyards were all closed down. This is what one man remembered about that time,

"Everybody was heartbroken and couldn't believe it when the big overhead cranes were dismantled. It really went home that this was the end.".

Workers who lost their jobs were not allowed **dole** money for long. They had to pass a Means Test and sell their furniture if they wanted to stay on the dole,

"We were means tested. Officers came to the house to inspect us. They said, 'sell that piano, you're well off'. Anything that was good in the house they would tell you to sell before they gave you any money.".

What do you think this man is thinking about his life 'on the dole'?

Means Test

A test carried out by the government on unemployed people to see if they really need the dole.

Dole

Money given to unemployed people who had passed the means test. It was to help them survive.

The Hunger Marches

Many people without jobs joined the National Unemployed Workers' Movement. They thought of ways of telling the rest of the country about their difficulties. Remember there was no television when these photographs were taken.

Groups of marchers walked from all the areas where there were no jobs. They all met for a big **rally** in London.

The most famous march was the Jarrow **Crusade**.

Look at these pictures of hunger marchers in the 1930s.

- ♦ Where did these marchers come from?
- ♦ What time of year do you think it was?
- ♦ How did they keep their spirits up?
- ♦ Why did they call the march a 'crusade'?
- ♦ Why was it important to have the photo taken?

Rally

A meeting.

Crusade

A journey which people go on if they believe strongly in something.

♦ **What message did these men carry on their banner?**

One Jarrow marcher remembers that there was another point of view,

"The well-offs actually booked windows in some of the West End hotels so they could have a first-class view of the people from the north who marched all the way down south to protest against their hunger."

This painting shows some rich Londoners looking out from inside a warm room.

♦ **Do you think they understand what the march is all about?**

♦ **How has the artist managed to make a point about the difference between living in Jarrow and living in London in 1936?**

Moving Away from Home

Some families in the depressed areas of Britain had to make a difficult decision. They had to leave their homes and their friends to look for work somewhere else.

These men are learning about farming.

♦ **What do you think they are being told?**

Some people were given a smallholding. They could rent a house and piece of land at a low rent. They had to grow enough food on the land for their own use and also some to sell at the market. First they had to learn about farming.

Many families left Ireland in the 1930s. Some of them wanted to find new jobs. Others wanted to leave the 'troubles' behind. The 'troubles' was the fighting between the Protestants and the Catholics. Both of these religious groups wanted to make the laws in Ireland but only the Protestants had the right to do so.

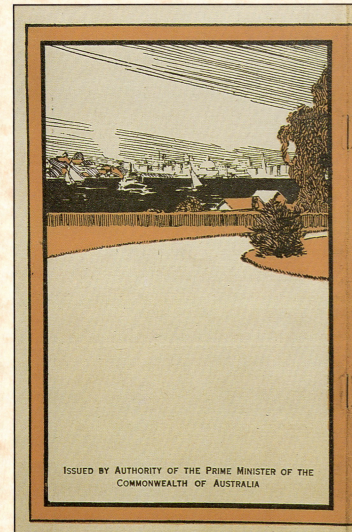

ISSUED BY AUTHORITY OF THE PRIME MINISTER OF THE
COMMONWEALTH OF AUSTRALIA

AUSTRALIA INVITES THE BRITISH DOMESTIC GIRL

Some single people emigrated to Australia. They only had to pay £10 for their fare. The rest was paid by the Australian government as the country needed more workers.

◆ **Why do you think that people listened to adverts like the one above?**

◆ **What sort of workers were they looking for?**

Some Welsh miners decided to go and join a war in Spain. They did not really want to go but if they did, at least they got paid for fighting. You can read more about the war in Spain on page 24.

Can you read some of the information on Tom Evans' paybook.

◆ **How old was he when he went to fight in Spain?**

◆ **Where did he come from?**

◆ **What was his job in Wales?**

New Buildings
and Jobs

New Buildings

At the same time but in different parts of Britain, business was booming and towns were expanding.

The pictures on these two pages show some new buildings put up in the 1930s. Many people thought they were too modern and did not like them because they looked so different. Today they are easy to recognise as a 1930s style, which is sometimes called the **art deco** style.

This is a photograph of the Hoover factory which was built in London in 1931. Find:

♦ the white stonework.

♦ the rounded pillars.

♦ the symmetry in the design.

♦ the rectangular metal windows.

Art Deco

A style of design popular in the 1930s. The designs had more straight lines than curved lines.

More stations were built on the London Underground in the 1930s.

Look at the inside of Acton station.

♦ **What is 'modern' about it?**

♦ **What clues do both buildings provide about the changes in the way of life in the 1930s?**

The British Broadcasting Corporation or BBC was started at the end of 1922. They moved to this brand new building in 1932. There they were able to make many more programmes. The building was very up-to-date.

This is where visitors went in. The studios were upstairs and in the basement.

♦ **What do you think any visitors thought about the BBC?**

Before 1930 most children had only had one school in their area. However in the 1930s, the government wanted to build secondary schools for everyone.

Many Councils decided to build in the new style of architecture because they thought that schools should be light and airy.

This is one of the schools built in the 1930s.

♦ **What do you think of this school?**

♦ **Is it like yours?**

♦ **What is different from yours?**

Electricity

One of the things which changed people's lives most in the 1930s was electricity.

A national grid system of cables and pylons, like the one below, was built. Many new power stations were opened. Between 1931 and 1936 twice as much electricity was available. It was made from coal, not nuclear fuels as it is today.

People liked using it. It was a clean fuel because it made no smoke and could be switched on and off. By 1937 nine million people had electricity in their homes or places where they worked. Fifteen years before only 2 million had been '**on the grid**'.

'On the grid'
Connected to the electricity supply.

Electricity made a big difference everywhere. Out in the street, the lighting was brighter. Traffic lights and cinemas were built. More electric trams were introduced.

The new factories could use machines driven by electricity. There was a big demand for new electrical goods. Making these provided new jobs. Electric engines replaced the steam trains on some lines. People bought electric irons, toasters, stoves, vacuum cleaners, and other appliances for their homes.

◆ How many things can you see in this advertisement?

◆ Why do you think the woman is called 'Miss Magnet'?

The advertisement says this is an 'Ideal' home.

◆ What does this tell you about the homes of the people the advertisers want to attract?

Suburbia

The ideal home in the Miss Magnet advertisement may have been in one of the new suburbs. Do you remember the houses in the background of the picture on page 3? Four million new homes were built in Britain between 1918 and 1938.

Some were built by the Council like these houses in Manchester. They replaced some of the old Victorian houses which had become unhealthy.

Look at the grass verges and the trees. The homes were for people with young families.

♦ How well designed do you think the estate was?

♦ What else did the families need?

Some people's ideas of an ideal home in the 1930s were houses like this one. They were designed in a more modern style like the buildings on pages 12 and 13.

What do you think of:

♦ the plain design?

♦ the flat roofs?

♦ the white breeze blocks?

♦ the metal windows?

♦ the balcony?

Many people became home owners in the 1930s. They bought homes like these with a mortgage. This meant that they paid money each week to a Building Society. After about 25 years they owned the houses.

Here is the advertisement for the houses when they were first built.

♦ What did the advertisers want the people to think about the houses?

♦ Who did they want to live in them?

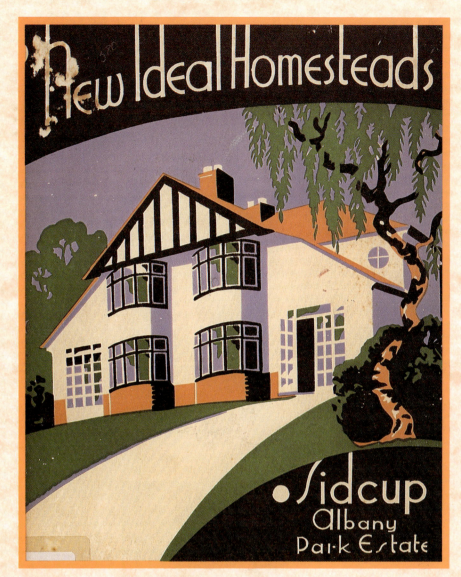

And here are the same houses today.

Look carefully at the photograph.

♦ Has anything been changed since they were first built?

♦ Are there any houses like these near where you live?

Transport

Wherever you lived it was nice to get out and about. Most people found they could afford to buy a bicycle in the 1930s.

Motorbikes were also popular and both men and women bought them. Children sometimes rode in a sidecar fixed to the bike.

How much like the bicycles of today does this one look?

Cars were much cheaper than they are today, but they were still too expensive for most families. Most cars were built in Britain then. There are still people alive today who can remember driving an Austin or a Morris.

Although there was not much traffic on the roads the first speed limit of 30mph (about 50km/hr) in towns was introduced in 1935.

♦ How is this car different from ones you see today?

♦ What sort of person was this advertisement aimed at?

Public transport was much better than it is today. Even people who had a car or bicycle used the bus or train to get from place to place.

Most towns had their own railway station and fares were cheap. Many people started to commute from their homes in the suburbs to an office in the city.

Find:
- ♦ the trains.
- ♦ the station.
- ♦ the people commuting.

In the country a proper bus service improved people's lives. Sometimes when they wanted to go for a day out they hired a charabanc like the one in this picture.

Better transport made going on holiday easier. In 1938 the government passed a new law which gave most people the right to have a holiday with pay for the first time in history.

The Wireless

In October 1936 the BBC started a television service but as hardly anyone had a set at home, few people were able to watch it.

At home everyone listened to the radio, or the wireless as it was called then. They listened on a set that looked like this.

Everyone wanted one and if they were short of money they bought one on hire purchase. Their favourite programmes were something like ours. Popular music, such as the songs of Gracie Fields and dance band music, comedy shows with stars like Wilfred Pickles and Elsie and Doris Waters, children's programmes and news from round the world were all popular.

This is a painting of Gracie Fields; she was a popular singer in the 1930s.

The Cinema

The cinema provided entertainment outside the home. People called it 'going to the pictures'. Most of the films were made in Hollywood in America. They showed glamorous stars like Greta Garbo and Douglas Fairbanks and comedians like Charlie Chaplin and Laurel and Hardy. All the films were in black and white photography.

A man called Walt Disney then discovered how to make cartoon films. They were in colour! The first big Disney film was made in 1938. It was the story of Snow White and the Seven Dwarfs.

Many of the films people liked in the 1930s are now on video. Perhaps you have seen some? You could talk about the films to someone who is over 70 and who may have seen them for the first time in a cinema like the one above.

Every Saturday morning the cinemas opened for children only. The programmes only cost a penny and were very popular.

Have you ever seen a Laurel and Hardy film on television?

People and Events

The Royal Family

The large number of wireless sets made it possible for the first time in history for the Royal family to talk directly to ordinary people in their homes.

King George **V** was our Queen's grandfather. He started the tradition of the Royal Christmas broadcast in 1932. This photograph shows him making that broadcast.

When he was dying in 1936, the wireless played only sad music and repeated these words at regular intervals; "The king's life is moving peacefully towards its close".

Why do you think this happened?

Was it because the BBC wanted to make the best use of the wireless to provide information or because they thought people wanted to feel that they were actually in the king's bedroom?

This stamp celebrates his Silver Jubilee, 1910–1935.

This is the Roman number 5. Roman numbers are usually used when talking about kings and queens.

The Abdication

After the death of King George V, his son became king, but he was never crowned. He **abdicated** from the throne in December 1936. This was because he wanted to marry an American called Wallis Simpson. She had been divorced and, in those days, many people thought that this made her an unsuitable person to become Queen.

King Edward VIII announced his plan to marry Mrs Simpson and to give up the throne on the wireless. This is what he said.

> "I cannot discharge my duties as king without the help and support of the woman I love.".

When Edward abdicated his brother, Queen Elizabeth's father, was crowned king.

This picture shows Edward making the speech. Many people at the time thought that Edward should have been allowed to be king and marry Wallis.

◆ **What do you think?**

Pictures like this one of Edward and Wallis appeared in newspapers of the time.

This stamp was one of only a few made of Edward when he was king.

Abdicated
To abdicate means to give up the position of king or queen by choice.

This is a picture of a Nazi flag. The Nazis were a group of German fascists.

Fascism

All through the 1930s, the news on the wireless and in the newspapers reported the activities of groups of people in Britain and Europe who called themselves fascists.

Their leaders were Adolf Hitler in Germany, Mussolini in Italy, General Franco in Spain, and Oswald Mosley in Britain. Their idea was that some races and nations were greater than others. To show how great they were, the fascists thought they would take over all the countries and people they thought were weaker than themselves.

The fascists had many supporters but lots of their ideas were evil. They wanted to kill Jews and other groups of people. There were many ugly clashes in Britain and Spain between fascists and anti-fascists and in Spain there was even a Civil War. Some Britons, like the Welsh miner Tom Glyn Evans, whose paybook you saw on page 11, joined the **International Brigade** to fight there.

This photograph shows the two fascist leaders Hitler and Mussolini at a big rally. It was taken in 1937. The two leaders called it a 'peace demonstration'.

In his books and speeches Hitler often said that Germany needs more 'lebensraum'. This was German for 'living space'. Many people knew this meant he wanted to extend his empire to the whole of Europe.

Look carefully at the picture.

♦ How are the leaders dressed?

♦ What message is Mussolini giving with his raised arm?

♦ Can you see any peace symbols, such as doves?

♦ Can you see any fascist badges called swastikas?

What do you think people living in 1937 thought about the fascists when they saw this photograph in their newspapers?

International Brigade

An army made up of people from many countries who wanted to defeat the fascist army in Spain.

Different Points of View

All over Britain people had different points of view about events in Europe. Some families welcomed Jewish **refugee** children who had been sent to Britain by their parents for safety. Hitler wanted to take all Jews in Europe from their homes and put them into prison camps. Some Jewish families managed to escape to Britain. Here are some arriving in Southampton

Some people called themselves the British Union of Fascists and marched in support of Hilter. They were called the 'blackshirts' because of the uniform they chose for themselves.

These are the 'blackshirts' at a rally. Find:

♦ the people watching. What are they doing?

Refugee

A person who is forced to leave their own home and has nowhere to go.

Some people called themselves **pacifists**. They said they would never fight a war again because of the millions of soldiers who had been killed in the First World War between 1914 and 1918.

These people marched for peace. They put things like gas masks over their faces. They wanted to frighten people about gas attacks if war came.

♦ What have they written on their banners?

On November 11, the day when red poppies are laid on war memorials to honour those who died in the wars, the Women's Cooperative Guild laid some white poppies. They said these were to remind people to work for peace, not war.

They also went on peace marches with their children. Can you see the white poppies on their banners?

The Prime Minister, Mr Chamberlain said the best thing to do was for him to go and talk to Mr Hitler 'face to face' and persuade him not to take his army into other European countries.

If you had been alive in 1938, which point of view would you have supported?

Pacifist

A person strongly against any war.

Talking to the Germans

Find:

♦ the piece of paper.

♦ the microphones that he spoke in to.

In 1938 Mr Chamberlain went to Munich to talk to the Germans. Hitler said that he would take over parts of Czechoslovakia, because many people spoke German there. Mr Chamberlain agreed with him.

What he did not know was that Hitler wanted to take over the parts where the people did not speak German and wanted to remain a country of their own.

When he landed back in Britain, huge crowds waited to welcome him. They cheered when he got off the aircraft and he agreed to make a speech.

He waved a small piece of paper for the crowd to see. He said it had been signed by himself and Hitler. It was an agreement that Britain and Germany would never go to war again. Mr Chamberlain said,

"I have brought back peace in our time.".

Portugal

Look at this map of Europe. Find:

♦ Germany.

♦ Austria. Hitler was invited into Austria in 1938.

♦ Czechoslovakia. Hitler invaded the country in 1939.

♦ Poland. This was the next country Hitler invaded.

♦ Belgium. Hitler threatened to invade there too.

Where do you think he wanted to go after that?

Six months later Hitler's army took control of the whole of Czechoslovakia. In a speech he said,

"Czechoslovakia has ceased to exist.".

Then Hitler took his army into Poland. The governments of Britain and France told Hitler to move his army out of Poland. If he did not they said they would have to declare war.

War is Declared

Sunday September 3rd 1939 was a pleasant sunny day. Many families were out in their gardens or waiting for their Sunday dinner. They had been told to keep their wireless sets on.

This is how one woman from Huddersfield remembers the day,

> "We were expecting the announcement on the radio and we were all in the living room, sitting there listening to it. Mother started to cry and father, who had been in the First World War, was very upset at the thought of any of his children having to go. I always remember him saying, 'I'd give my right arm rather than have any of you go through what I went through in the First World War'. It was very emotional of course.".

At 11.15 a.m. Mr Chamberlain spoke on the wireless. This is what he said,

> "I have to tell you that this country is now at war with Germany.".

Half an hour later, the **sirens** sounded in London, to warn people that an air raid attack was about to happen.

This is what the paper said about the war beginning.

Siren

A warning sound in the street. A bit like the sound of a police car today.

The outbreak of war brought many changes to people's lives and to the places where they lived. It was the end of the decade we call the 1930s.

Free air raid shelters were given to families in all the big cities. These had to be put up in the back garden in case the Germans started dropping bombs. Sandbags were put round all the biggest buildings.

Soldiers were put on trains to go to France. By September 27th fifteen thousand had arrived in France.

Find:

♦ the air raid shelters.

♦ the men giving them out.

What sort of mood do you think these soldiers are in?

♦ What are they thinking about the outbreak of war?

♦ Find Berlin on the map on page 29.

♦ What is the musical instrument for?

♦ Why was the photograph taken?

All across Europe, children had to leave their homes.

These women and children arrived by ship in Britain. They had escaped from the Germans in Poland. Do you think they really want to be in Britain?

These British children were sent from the city into the country. They are carrying their gas masks over their shoulders.

What do you think they are all feeling about the war?